J
567.914
GRA

Gray, Susan Heinrichs

Iguanodon

INTRODUCING DINOSAURS

IGUANODON

BY SUSAN H. GRAY · ILLUSTRATED BY ROBERT SQUIER

The Child's World

Published by The Child's World®
1980 Lookout Drive • Mankato, MN 56003-1705
800-599-READ • www.childsworld.com

ACKNOWLEDGMENTS
The Child's World®: Mary Berendes, Publishing Director
The Design Lab: Kathleen Petelinsek, Art Direction and Design;
Victoria Stanley and Anna Petelinsek, Page Production
Editorial Directions: E. Russell Primm, Editor; Lucia Raatma, Copy Editor;
Dina Rubin, Proofreader; Tim Griffin, Indexer

PHOTO CREDITS
©Broker/Dreamstime.com: cover, 2–3; ©Getty Images/Hulton Arcive:
14–15; ©Photo Researchers/Science Photo Library: 16 (top) (Chris Butler);
American Museum of Natural History: 16 (bottom); ©Royal Belgian
Institute of Natural Sciences/Thierry Hubin: 17; ©Scott Lewis/Alamy: 18–19

LIBRARY OF CONGRESS CATALOGING-IN-PUBLICATION DATA
Gray, Susan Heinrichs.
  Iguanodon / by Susan H. Gray; illustrated by Robert Squier.
    p. cm.—(Introducing dinosaurs)
  Includes bibliographical references and index.
  ISBN 978-1-60253-238-0 (lib. bound: alk. paper)
  1. Iguanodon—Juvenile literature. I. Squier, Robert, ill. II. Title. III. Series.
  QE862.O65G74552 2009
  567.914—dc22   2009001625

Printed in the United States of America • Mankato, MN
September 2010 • PA02076

TABLE OF CONTENTS

WHAT WAS IGUANODON?

Iguanodon (ig-WA-nuh-don) was a big, plant-eating dinosaur. It was one of the first dinosaurs ever discovered.

Iguanodon *was heavy. It weighed about as much as two pickup trucks!*

6

WHAT DID *IGUANODON* LOOK LIKE?

Iguanodon was enormous. It could have weighed as much as two pickup trucks! It had giant legs and large arms. Its tail was big and heavy.

Iguanodon's tail was important. Without it, Iguanodon would have lost its balance and fallen over.

Instead of thumbs, *Iguanodon* had **spikes**. Instead of lips, it had a beak like a turtle. It had no teeth in the front of its mouth. All of its teeth were along the sides of its mouth.

Iguanodon's beak and teeth were perfect for eating plants. It used the flat teeth in the back of its mouth to chew.

WHAT DID *IGUANODON* DO ALL DAY?

Iguanodon probably never spent a day alone. Instead, it lived and traveled in a **herd**. The group slowly plodded along. Some walked on two feet and some on four. When the herd found food, they all stopped to eat. *Iguanodon* ate leaves, twigs, bushes, and ferns.

Traveling in a herd helped protect Iguanodon. *Any attacking dinosaur would be outnumbered.*

Sometimes, *Iguanodon* rose up on its hind legs. Then it could reach higher branches. It clipped them off with its hard beak. It ground everything up with its cheek teeth.

After a meal, *Iguanodon* probably took a nap. In the herd, there was safety. Some of the dinosaurs could always watch for danger. If another dinosaur attacked, it was in for a surprise. *Iguanodon* could stab an attacker with its thumb spikes!

Iguanodon *could fight if it needed to. Its thumb spikes were sharp!*

14

HOW DO WE KNOW ABOUT *IGUANODON*?

About 200 years ago, no one knew about *Iguanodon*. No one even knew about dinosaurs! Then people began finding **fossils**. Some *Iguanodon* teeth were found in 1823. Then some bones and thumb spikes were found. No one knew what kind of animal they came from.

In 1878, coal miners in Belgium found the bones of 30 Iguanodon.

One person said the fossils were from a **rhinoceros**. Another said they were from a big **lizard**. Another said they were from a giant fish! Finally, everyone decided the fossils were from a strange, **ancient** animal. They called that animal a dinosaur.

Mary Ann Mantell (top) is thought to have discovered the first Iguanodon fossil. Her husband, Gideon Mantell (bottom), spent his whole life studying fossils. He was one of the first people to study dinosaurs. Many Iguanodon bones are on display in this museum in Belgium (far right).

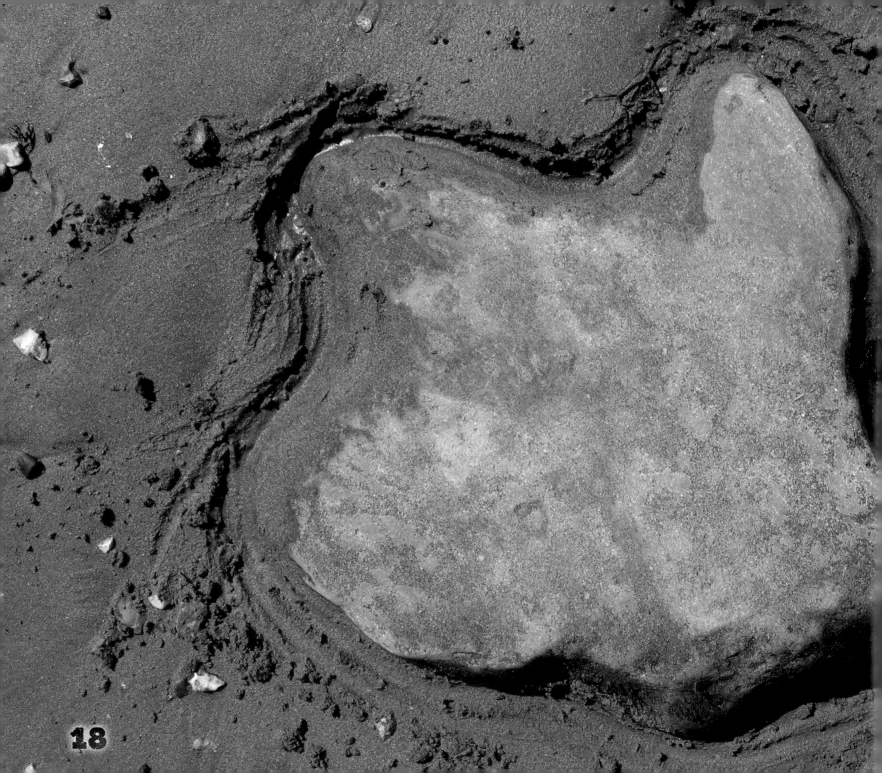

WHAT ELSE DID *IGUANODON* LEAVE BEHIND?

Scientists have found many *Iguanodon* fossils. They have found bones, skulls, and teeth. In one place, they found about 30 *Iguanodons* together! In other places, they have found *Iguanodon* footprints. *Iguanodon* left lots of fossils behind!

Iguanodon *footprints can teach us many things. Scientists can use them to guess how fast* Iguanodon *moved and where it lived.*

WHERE HAVE IGUANODON BONES BEEN FOUND?

South Dakota

Utah

Belgium

Germany

Mongolia

England

EUROPE

ASIA

NORTH AMERICA

Spain

Atlantic Ocean

Pacific Ocean

Tunisia

AFRICA

SOUTH AMERICA

Indian Ocean

AUSTRALIA

Map Key

Where *Iguanodon* bones have been found

Where possible *Iguanodon* fossils or tracks have been found

Southern Ocean

WHO FINDS THE BONES?

Fossil hunters find dinosaur bones. Some fossil hunters are scientists. Others are people who hunt fossils for fun. They go to areas where dinosaurs once lived. They find bones in rocky places, in mountainsides, and in deserts.

When fossil hunters discover dinosaur bones, they get busy. They use picks to chip rocks away from the fossils. They use small brushes to sweep off any dirt. They take pictures of the fossils. They also write notes about where the fossils were found. They want to remember everything!

Fossil hunters use many tools to dig up fossils. It is very important to use the right tools so the fossils do not get damaged.

GLOSSARY

ancient (*AYN-shunt*) Ancient things are those that existed a very long time ago.

fossils (*FOSS-ullz*) Fossils are preserved parts of plants and animals that died long ago.

herd (*HURD*) A herd is a group of animals that travel together.

Iguanodon (*ig-WA-nuh-don*) *Iguanodon* was a dinosaur that ate plants.

lizard (*LIZ-urd*) A lizard is a scaly animal that walks on four legs.

rhinoceros (*rye-NOSS-ur-uss*) A rhinoceros is a large animal with thick skin and two horns on its snout.

scientists (*SY-un-tists*) Scientists are people who study how things work through observations and experiments.

spikes (*SPIKES*) Spikes are large, sharp, pointed things.

BOOKS

Johnson, Jinny. *Iguanodon and Other Plant-eating Dinosaurs.*
London: Franklin Watts Ltd., 2007.

Parker, Steve. *Dinosaurus: The Complete Guide to Dinosaurs.*
New York: Firefly Books, 2003.

Schomp, Virginia. *Iguanodon and Other Spiky-thumbed Plant-eaters.*
Tarrytown, NY: Benchmark Books, 2006.

Vecchia, Fabio Marco Dalla. *Iguanodon.*
San Diego, CA: Blackbirch Press, 2007.

WEB SITES

Visit our Web site for lots of links about *Iguanodon*:
CHILDSWORLD.COM/LINKS

Note to Parents, Teachers, and Librarians: We routinely verify our Web links to make sure they are safe, active sites—so encourage your readers to check them out!

INDEX

ABOUT THE AUTHOR

Susan Gray has written more than ninety books for children. She especially likes to write about animals. Susan lives in Cabot, Arkansas, with her husband, Michael, and many pets.

ABOUT THE ILLUSTRATOR

Robert Squier has been drawing dinosaurs ever since he could hold a crayon. Today, instead of using crayons, he uses pencils, paint, and the computer. Robert lives in New Hampshire with his wife, Jessica, and a house full of dinosaur toys. *Stegosaurus* is his favorite dinosaur.